JOE GILBERT

Lead Generation Unlocked

First edition

This book was professionally typeset on Reedsy.
Find out more at reedsy.com

Contents

I

Foreword

"Within the vast digital landscape of the web, lies the incredible limitless power to attract, engage, and transform visitors into loyal clients."

– Joe Gilbert

1

About the Author

Joe Gilbert is a seasoned expert in the field of digital marketing, renowned for his exceptional insights and innovative strategies. With a passion for helping businesses thrive in the digital age, Joe has dedicated his career to transforming online marketing into a powerful tool for lead generation and business growth.

In 2018, Joe founded Red Giraffe, a multi-award winning digital marketing agency that has quickly become a recognised name in the industry. Under his leadership, Red Giraffe has consistently delivered outstanding results for clients across various sectors, from startups to established corporations. The agency's commitment to excellence has earned them numerous accolades and industry awards, solidifying their reputation as leaders in the digital marketing space.

Joe's expertise in digital marketing is not just a product of professional success but is also grounded in his academic background. He holds a Master's degree in International Marketing, which he obtained from Edinburgh Napier University, where he honed his strategic thinking and developed a deep understanding of global market dynamics. This unique blend of practical experience and academic knowledge sets Joe apart as a thought leader in the field.

Beyond his professional achievements, Joe Gilbert is known for his commitment to mentorship and education within the digital marketing community. He has mentored aspiring marketers and has been an advocate for ethical and sustainable marketing practices.

In this book, Joe leverages his extensive experience and expertise to guide readers on the journey to turning their websites into lead generation machines. With a wealth of practical knowledge and real-world success stories, he empowers readers to navigate the complex world of digital marketing with confidence, ultimately helping them achieve their business goals.

"Unlock the secrets to website lead generation and take your business to new heights with the insights and strategies shared in this book. I'm excited to be your guide on this transformative journey." - Joe Gilbert

2

The Myth of the Expensive Online Brochure

In today's fast-paced digital landscape, your website should be more than just an online presence. It should be a dynamic and powerful tool—a lead generation machine that propels your business forward. Yet, for many, this vision remains unfulfilled. For far too long, websites have been trapped in the role of expensive online brochures, serving as little more than static placeholders on the vast canvas of the internet.

As you embark on this journey to transform your website into a lead generation powerhouse, it's essential to confront the harsh reality that many businesses face. The myth of the expensive online brochure persists, and it's time to dispel it once and for all.

Imagine this scenario: You've invested substantial resources into building a beautiful website. It's visually appealing, laden with captivating images, and filled with eloquent descriptions of your products or services. It's a digital work of art, and you couldn't be prouder of it. But there's one problem—it's not generating leads, and it's certainly not driving sales.

If this scenario sounds familiar, you're not alone. Countless businesses find themselves in a similar predicament. They've spent substantial sums on website development, only to discover that their online presence does little to contribute to their bottom line. It's a frustrating and all-too-common reality.

Why does this happen? How can a beautifully designed website fail so miserably at its core purpose? The answer lies in the misconception that a website is a one-time investment, a digital business card, or an online portfolio. This limited perspective overlooks the true potential of the digital realm and underestimates the profound impact a strategically designed and optimized website can have on your business.

In this book, we will embark on a journey to uncover the untapped potential of your website. We'll explore the strategies, techniques, and mindset shifts necessary to turn your website into a lead generation machine that drives growth and success. But before we delve into the strategies and tactics, it's crucial to understand why so many websites fall short.

Let's dissect the myth of the expensive online brochure and the key reasons why most websites fail to deliver the results businesses crave:

1. Lack of Purpose: Many websites lack a clear and well-defined purpose. They may look appealing, but they don't have a specific goal in mind, whether it's capturing leads, making sales, or nurturing prospects.

2. Ineffective Content: Beautiful visuals and eloquent descriptions are important, but they're not enough. Content must resonate with your target audience, address their pain points, and guide them toward taking action.

3. Ignoring User Experience: User experience (UX) plays a pivotal role in determining how visitors interact with your website. If your site is difficult to navigate or doesn't load quickly, you're likely losing potential leads.

4. Neglecting SEO: Without proper search engine optimization (SEO), your website may remain buried in the vast online landscape, making it virtually invisible to potential customers.

5. Failing to Capture Leads: Many websites don't have effective lead capture mechanisms in place, missing out on opportunities to engage and nurture potential customers.

Over the chapters that follow, we will address these issues and provide actionable strategies to transform your website into a lead generation machine. It's time to shatter the myth of the expensive online brochure and unlock the true potential of your digital presence. Your website can be more than just a pretty face; it can be a driving force behind your business's success. Are you ready to embark on this transformative journey? Let's get started.

Bonus content: *Want to know what's holding your website back from online success? Visit https://red-giraffe.com/ebook/leads for* *your free website audit*

3

Defining Your Lead Generation Goals

In the realm of digital marketing, setting clear and achievable goals is the compass that guides your journey. Your website's transformation into a lead generation machine begins with a well-defined destination. Without a destination, you risk wandering aimlessly through the vast landscape of the internet, uncertain of where you're headed or how to measure success.

The Power of Clear Objectives

Imagine embarking on a road trip without a destination in mind. You fill your gas tank, pack your bags, and hit the road, but you have no idea where you're going. It's an adventure, sure, but it's also a recipe for frustration and wasted resources.

Your website's journey is no different. Without clear lead generation goals, your efforts may lack direction and purpose. Your website might look good, but is it serving its intended purpose? Is it helping your business grow? These questions can only be answered when you define your goals.

What Are Lead Generation Goals?

Lead generation goals are specific, measurable, and attainable objectives that define what you want your website to achieve. These goals serve as the foundation upon which your entire lead generation strategy is built. They provide focus, motivation, and a means to gauge progress.

Your lead generation goals should align with your overall business objectives. They can encompass various aspects of your website's performance, such as:

1. **Lead Acquisition:** How many leads do you aim to capture through your website in a given period?
2. **Conversion Rate:** What percentage of your website visitors do you want to convert into leads?
3. **Sales Revenue:** What revenue target do you hope to achieve through your website-generated leads?
4. **Audience Growth:** Are you looking to expand your website's reach and increase traffic from your target audience?
5. **Customer Engagement:** Do you want to foster stronger relationships with your existing customers through your website?

The SMART Approach to Goal Setting

To ensure your lead generation goals are effective, use the SMART criteria:

- **Specific:** Your goals should be well-defined and clear. Vague objectives leave room for misinterpretation and confusion.
- **Measurable:** There should be a quantifiable way to track progress toward your goals. If you can't measure it, you

can't manage it.

- **Achievable:** Set realistic goals that can be accomplished within your resources and timeframe. Unrealistic goals can lead to frustration and burnout.
- **Relevant:** Your goals should align with your business objectives and contribute to your overall success.
- **Time-Bound:** Establish a deadline for achieving your goals. Having a timeframe creates a sense of urgency and accountability.

Example: Setting Lead Generation Goals

Let's say you run a small e-commerce business selling handmade jewelry. Your website currently generates 200 monthly visitors, and you capture an average of 10 leads (newsletter sign-ups) each month. Your goal might be to double your lead capture rate within the next six months.

This goal follows the SMART criteria:

- **Specific:** Doubling the lead capture rate.
- **Measurable:** From 10 leads to 20 leads per month.
- **Achievable:** Given your current traffic and conversion rates, it's a realistic goal.
- **Relevant:** More leads can lead to increased sales.
- **Time-Bound:** Achieving it in six months provides a clear deadline.

Defining your lead generation goals is the crucial first step toward turning your website into a lead generation machine. With a destination in mind, you'll have a roadmap for the chapters ahead, where we'll delve into strategies and tactics to help you achieve those objectives.

4

Understanding Your Target Audience

Your journey to transforming your website into a lead generation powerhouse continues with a critical step: understanding your target audience. In the digital landscape, where attention spans are short and competition is fierce, knowing your audience intimately can be the key to capturing their attention and converting them into leads.

Why Audience Understanding Matters

Imagine trying to strike up a conversation with a group of people without knowing anything about them. You might stumble, say the wrong things, and struggle to connect. The same principle applies to your website and its visitors. Without a deep understanding of your target audience, your website's content and messaging may miss the mark, leaving potential leads disinterested or confused.

To create content that resonates and drives conversions, you need to answer essential questions about your audience:

- Who are they?
- What are their needs, desires, and pain points?
- How do they prefer to consume information?
- What motivates them to take action?
- Where do they hang out online?

Creating Customer Personas

One effective way to gain insights into your audience is by creating customer personas, which are fictional representations of your ideal customers. These personas should be based on research and data, providing a clear picture of different segments of your audience. You can start by gathering information from sources such as surveys, social media analytics, and customer feedback.

Each customer persona should include:

1. **Demographic Information:** Age, gender, location, income, job title, etc.
2. **Psychographic Insights:** Interests, values, lifestyle, and attitudes.
3. **Behavioral Traits:** Online behavior, buying habits, preferred communication channels.
4. **Pain Points:** The problems or challenges they face that your product or service can solve.
5. **Goals and Objectives:** What they hope to achieve, both personally and professionally.

Tailoring Your Website Content

Once you've developed customer personas, use them as a guiding force in crafting your website content and messaging.

Tailor your content to address the specific needs and interests of each persona. For example, if you have identified two distinct customer personas for your handmade jewelry business—one being fashion-conscious teenagers and the other being eco-conscious adults—you might create separate content and marketing campaigns that speak directly to each group's unique preferences and values.

User-Centered Design

Understanding your target audience also influences your website's design. User-centered design principles ensure that your website's layout, navigation, and user experience cater to the preferences and behaviors of your audience. Consider factors like mobile responsiveness, page load times, and intuitive navigation, all of which can impact how well your website engages visitors.

Iterative Learning

Audience understanding is not a one-time task but an ongoing process. As your business evolves and your audience changes, so should your customer personas and content strategies. Regularly review and update your personas, conduct surveys, and analyze user data to stay aligned with your audience's shifting preferences and needs.

By delving deep into the minds and hearts of your target audience, you'll be well-equipped to create a website that not only attracts visitors but also converts them into leads. In the upcoming chapters, we'll explore how to leverage this understanding to craft compelling content, design user-friendly experiences, and implement strategies that resonate with your audience's motivations and goals.

5

Crafting Compelling Content

With a clear understanding of your target audience in place, it's time to dive into the heart of lead generation—compelling content. Your website's content is the bridge that connects you with your audience, offering valuable information, solving their problems, and ultimately enticing them to become leads.

The Role of Content in Lead Generation

Think of your website's content as the conversation starter in the digital world. Just as engaging in meaningful dialogue with someone can lead to a deeper connection, compelling content can initiate a relationship between your business and your website visitors. It's the foundation upon which trust and credibility are built.

But what exactly makes content compelling? It's a combination of several factors:

1. **Relevance:** Content should directly address the needs and interests of your target audience. It should provide

solutions to their problems or offer valuable insights.

2. **Clarity:** Compelling content is easy to understand. It conveys its message concisely and effectively, avoiding jargon or unnecessary complexity.

3. **Engagement:** Content should capture the reader's attention and keep them interested. It can do this through storytelling, relatable examples, or a conversational tone.

4. **Value:** Content should offer something of value to the reader. Whether it's information, entertainment, or inspiration, it should leave the audience feeling that they gained something from engaging with it.

5. **Action-Oriented:** Ultimately, compelling content should encourage the reader to take action, whether that's signing up for a newsletter, downloading a resource, or making a purchase.

Types of Compelling Content

There are various types of content you can create to engage your audience and generate leads. Some of the most effective include:

1. **Blog Posts:** Informative and educational articles that showcase your expertise and address common questions or pain points of your audience.

2. **Videos:** Engaging video content that can range from explainer videos to product demonstrations and customer testimonials.

3. **Infographics:** Visual representations of data or information that are easy to digest and share on social media.

4. **Ebooks and Whitepapers:** In-depth resources that provide valuable insights or solutions in exchange for contact

information (lead capture).

5. **Case Studies:** Real-life examples of how your product or service has helped customers solve problems and achieve their goals.

6. **Webinars and Live Events:** Live or recorded presentations, discussions, or workshops that offer interactivity and value to your audience.

Content Optimization

Creating compelling content is essential, but it's equally important to optimize it for both search engines and user experience. This involves:

- **Keyword Research:** Identifying relevant keywords and phrases to incorporate into your content to improve search engine visibility.
- **On-Page SEO:** Properly formatting content with headings, meta descriptions, and alt text for images.
- **User-Friendly Formatting:** Making content easy to skim with subheadings, bullet points, and short paragraphs.
- **Visuals and Multimedia:** Incorporating images, videos, and other multimedia elements to enhance engagement.

Content Calendar and Strategy

To maintain a consistent flow of compelling content, it's advisable to create a content calendar. This calendar outlines the topics, formats, and publication schedules for your content. It helps ensure that you stay on track and continue to provide value to your audience over time.

In the chapters that follow, we'll delve deeper into content creation strategies, distribution channels, and techniques for optimizing your website's content to convert visitors into leads. Crafting compelling content is an art and science, and it's one of the most powerful tools in your lead generation toolkit.

6

Website Design for Conversion

Your website's design plays a pivotal role in turning casual visitors into engaged leads. Beyond aesthetics, effective web design optimizes user experience and guides visitors toward taking desired actions. In this chapter, we'll explore the principles and strategies for designing a website that converts.

The Power of First Impressions

In the digital realm, first impressions are formed within milliseconds. Your website's design is the initial handshake, and it must convey professionalism, trustworthiness, and relevance. Here's how to make a positive first impression:

1. **Clean and Professional Look:** Keep your design clean and organized. Use professional imagery and consistent branding elements to build trust.
2. **Mobile Responsiveness:** Ensure your website is fully responsive to accommodate visitors on various devices, including smartphones and tablets.
3. **Loading Speed:** A slow-loading website can deter visitors.

Optimize images and minimize code to improve loading times.

4. **User-Friendly Navigation:** Create an intuitive navigation menu that makes it easy for visitors to find what they're looking for.

5. **Clear Calls to Action (CTAs):** Use visually appealing and persuasive CTAs to guide users toward taking specific actions, such as signing up for a newsletter or requesting a quote.

Conversion-Centric Design Elements

Effective web design goes beyond aesthetics; it should be conversion-centric. Here are essential design elements to focus on:

1. **Whitespace:** Allow for ample whitespace to prevent visual clutter and make content easier to digest.

2. **Typography:** Choose readable fonts and font sizes for your content, ensuring a consistent and accessible reading experience.

3. **Color Psychology:** Utilize color psychology to evoke emotions and reinforce your brand identity.

4. **Visual Hierarchy:** Use size, color, and placement to emphasize important elements, such as CTAs or key messages.

5. **Trust Indicators:** Incorporate trust-building elements, such as client testimonials, security badges, and industry certifications.

A/B Testing and User Feedback

Designing for conversion is an iterative process. Conduct A/B tests to compare different design variations and identify what resonates best with your audience. Additionally, gather user feedback through surveys, analytics, and usability testing to pinpoint areas for improvement.

Landing Pages for Lead Capture

Landing pages are a critical part of your website design when it comes to lead generation. These dedicated pages are designed to capture visitor information, such as email addresses, in exchange for valuable offers like ebooks, webinars, or free trials.

Key elements of an effective landing page include:

- A compelling headline that highlights the offer's value.
- A concise description of what the offer entails.
- A visually appealing image or graphic related to the offer.
- A clear and persuasive CTA that encourages visitors to take action.
- A simple lead capture form with as few fields as necessary.
- Trust-building elements, such as testimonials or privacy assurances.

User Experience (UX) Matters

A user-friendly and intuitive website not only enhances user experience but also boosts conversion rates. Consider the following UX principles:

- Intuitive navigation that guides visitors seamlessly through your site.
- Fast-loading pages to prevent visitors from bouncing due to slow load times.
- Mobile optimization to cater to the growing number of

mobile users.
- Accessibility features to make your site usable by all individuals, including those with disabilities.

In the upcoming chapters, we'll explore how to further optimize your website for lead generation, including strategies for effective SEO, social media integration, and email marketing. Your website's design is a crucial piece of the lead generation puzzle, as it sets the stage for all interactions with your audience.

7

The Power of Landing Pages in Lead Generation

Landing pages are a crucial component of any successful lead generation strategy. In this chapter, we'll explore what landing pages are, how they're used, and best practices for creating effective landing pages that convert visitors into leads.

What Are Landing Pages?

A landing page is a standalone web page created specifically for a marketing or advertising campaign. It's designed with a single, focused purpose: to encourage visitors to take a particular action. That action could be anything from signing up for a newsletter to requesting a demo, downloading an ebook, making a purchase, or filling out a contact form.

Unlike your website's homepage or other pages with multiple objectives, landing pages are streamlined and free from distractions. They typically include elements such as:

- A clear and compelling headline that aligns with the cam-

paign's message.
- A concise explanation of the offer or value proposition.
- A visually appealing layout and design.
- A call-to-action (CTA) that prompts visitors to take the desired action.
- A lead capture form to collect visitor information, such as name, email address, and other relevant details.
- Supporting visuals, such as images or videos, to enhance understanding.

How Are Landing Pages Used in Lead Generation?

Landing pages play a pivotal role in lead generation for several reasons:

1. **Focused Conversion:** Landing pages are designed to guide visitors toward a specific action, making it easier to convert them into leads or customers.
2. **Targeted Messaging:** You can tailor the messaging on a landing page to match the context of the marketing campaign or advertisement that led visitors there. This ensures consistency and relevance, increasing the likelihood of conversion.
3. **Lead Capture:** The lead capture form on a landing page allows you to collect valuable contact information from visitors, turning anonymous website traffic into identifiable leads.
4. **A/B Testing:** Landing pages are ideal for A/B testing, where you can create multiple versions with slight variations to determine which one performs better in terms of conversions.
5. **Analytics and Tracking:** Because landing pages have

a clear and specific purpose, it's easier to track their performance and measure the ROI of your marketing campaigns.

Best Practices for Effective Landing Pages:

Creating effective landing pages is an art and science. Here are some best practices to consider:

1. **Simplify and Focus:** Keep the content and design simple and focused on the main offer or action you want visitors to take.
2. **Compelling Headline:** Craft a clear and compelling headline that grabs visitors' attention and communicates the value of the offer.
3. **Clear Value Proposition:** Explain the benefits of the offer concisely and clearly, emphasizing how it solves a problem or meets a need.
4. **Eye-Catching Visuals:** Use high-quality images or videos that complement the message and enhance understanding.
5. **Concise Form:** Keep the lead capture form short and request only essential information. Longer forms can deter potential leads.
6. **Strong CTA:** Create an attention-grabbing CTA button with action-oriented text that encourages visitors to click and convert.
7. **Mobile Optimization:** Ensure that your landing page is fully responsive and user-friendly on mobile devices.
8. **Trust Signals:** Include trust-building elements such as testimonials, trust badges, and privacy assurances to build credibility.
9. **Remove Navigation:** Eliminate navigation links that can

distract visitors from the main goal of the page.

10. **A/B Testing:** Continuously test different elements, such as headlines, images, and CTAs, to optimize conversion rates.

Landing pages are a critical tool in lead generation, enabling you to capture and convert website visitors into valuable leads or customers. When used effectively and optimized over time, landing pages can significantly improve the success of your marketing campaigns and contribute to the growth of your business.

8

Implementing Effective SEO

Search Engine Optimization (SEO) is the cornerstone of online visibility and organic traffic. To transform your website into a lead generation machine, you must ensure that it ranks well in search engine results pages (SERPs). In this chapter, we'll delve into the strategies and techniques for implementing effective SEO.

The Importance of SEO in Lead Generation

SEO is the process of optimizing your website to rank higher in search engine results. When your website appears prominently in search results for relevant keywords, it attracts a steady stream of organic traffic. This organic traffic can then be converted into leads through well-crafted content and lead capture mechanisms.

Here are the primary components of effective SEO:

1. **Keyword Research:** Identify the keywords and phrases your target audience uses when searching for products

or services similar to yours. Tools like Google Keyword Planner can help you discover relevant keywords.

2. **On-Page SEO:** Optimize individual pages on your website for specific keywords. This involves optimizing titles, meta descriptions, headings, and content.

3. **Quality Content:** High-quality, informative, and engaging content not only attracts visitors but also encourages other websites to link to your content, boosting your SEO.

4. **Backlinks:** Acquire backlinks from authoritative and relevant websites in your industry. High-quality backlinks improve your website's credibility and authority.

5. **User Experience (UX):** User-friendly design and fast-loading pages contribute to a positive user experience, which can indirectly impact SEO.

6. **Mobile Optimization:** Given the increasing use of mobile devices, ensure that your website is mobile-responsive for better SEO performance.

Local SEO Considerations

For businesses with a physical presence or serving specific geographic areas, local SEO is paramount. It helps your website appear in local search results, such as "best restaurants near me" or "plumbers in [city]."

Key components of local SEO include:

- Creating and optimizing a Google My Business profile.
- Ensuring consistent NAP (Name, Address, Phone number) information across online directories.
- Generating positive online reviews from satisfied customers.

- Including location-specific keywords in your content.

Technical SEO

Technical SEO focuses on the backend aspects of your website that impact its search engine ranking. Key technical SEO considerations include:

- Site speed optimization for faster loading times.
- XML sitemap creation to help search engines index your content.
- Proper use of canonical tags to avoid duplicate content issues.
- Implementing schema markup to enhance search results with rich snippets.

Regular Monitoring and Analysis

SEO is an ongoing effort that requires continuous monitoring and analysis. Utilize tools like Google Analytics and Google Search Console to track your website's performance in search results. Regularly review your rankings, traffic patterns, and user behavior to make data-driven adjustments to your SEO strategy.

In the following chapters, we'll explore additional strategies to enhance your website's lead generation capabilities, including leveraging social media, email marketing, and conversion rate optimization (CRO). Effective SEO is a foundational element, ensuring that your website is discoverable by potential leads actively searching for your products or services online.

9

Leveraging PPC Advertising for Website Traffic and Lead Generation

Pay-Per-Click (PPC) advertising is a powerful digital marketing strategy that allows you to drive targeted traffic to your website quickly. In this chapter, we'll explore the benefits of PPC, how to get started, and best practices for using PPC to boost website traffic and lead generation.

What Is PPC Advertising?

PPC advertising is a digital marketing model where advertisers pay a fee each time their ad is clicked. It's a way to buy visits to your website rather than relying on organic traffic. PPC platforms, such as Google Ads and Bing Ads, enable businesses to bid on keywords relevant to their products or services and display ads to users searching for those keywords.

Benefits of Using PPC for Website Traffic and Lead Generation:

1. **Immediate Results:** PPC campaigns can be set up quickly, and you can start driving traffic to your website almost

immediately.

2. **Targeted Traffic:** You can choose specific keywords, demographics, locations, and even the time of day your ads are displayed, ensuring that your ads reach the right audience.

3. **Measurable Results:** PPC platforms provide detailed analytics and tracking, allowing you to measure the performance of your campaigns and calculate ROI.

4. **Budget Control:** You have control over your budget and can set daily or monthly spending limits, making PPC accessible for businesses of all sizes.

5. **Ad Testing:** PPC campaigns allow you to experiment with different ad copy, headlines, and visuals to determine what resonates best with your audience.

6. **Lead Generation:** By sending traffic to dedicated landing pages with lead capture forms, PPC can be a potent tool for generating leads.

Getting Started with PPC Advertising:

1. **Keyword Research:** Identify relevant keywords that align with your business and the products or services you offer. Use keyword research tools to discover popular and profitable keywords.

2. **Choose the Right PPC Platform:** Decide which PPC platform(s) align best with your goals. Google Ads is the most popular, but platforms like Bing Ads, Facebook Ads, and LinkedIn Ads may also be suitable depending on your target audience.

3. **Campaign Structure:** Organize your campaigns and ad groups logically. Each campaign should focus on a specific product, service, or goal, while ad groups should contain

closely related keywords.

4. **Compelling Ad Copy:** Craft persuasive ad copy that high-lights the unique selling points of your offering. Use ad extensions to provide additional information and encourage clicks.

5. **Landing Pages:** Create dedicated landing pages that match the message of your ads and guide visitors toward the desired action, whether it's signing up for a newsletter or making a purchase.

6. **Budget and Bidding:** Set your daily or monthly budget and choose a bidding strategy that aligns with your objectives, whether it's maximizing clicks, conversions, or ROI.

Best Practices for Successful PPC Campaigns:

1. **Quality Score:** Pay attention to your Quality Score, a metric used by Google Ads to measure the relevance and quality of your ads. Higher Quality Scores can lead to lower costs and better ad positions.

2. **Ad Extensions:** Use ad extensions to provide additional information, such as site links, callout extensions, and structured snippets, to make your ads more appealing.

3. **Negative Keywords:** Utilize negative keywords to filter out irrelevant traffic and ensure your ads are shown to the most relevant audience.

4. **Ad Testing:** Continuously test different ad variations to optimize click-through rates (CTR) and conversion rates.

5. **Conversion Tracking:** Implement conversion tracking to measure the effectiveness of your campaigns and under-stand which keywords and ads drive leads or sales.

6. **A/B Testing:** Experiment with different landing page

designs and content to improve conversion rates.

Monitoring and Optimization:

Once your PPC campaigns are live, ongoing monitoring and optimization are crucial:

- Regularly review campaign performance and adjust bidding strategies.
- Monitor click-through rates, conversion rates, and cost-per-conversion to identify areas for improvement.
- Test new keywords and ad copy to expand your reach and improve relevancy.
- Ensure your landing pages are user-friendly, load quickly, and provide a seamless user experience.
- Utilize remarketing to re-engage with visitors who didn't convert initially.

PPC advertising is a versatile and effective tool for driving targeted traffic to your website and generating leads. By following best practices, continuously monitoring performance, and optimizing your campaigns, you can leverage PPC to increase website traffic, attract potential leads, and grow your business online.

10

Exploring Different PPC Platforms for Your Advertising Campaigns

Pay-Per-Click (PPC) advertising offers various platforms to reach your target audience and promote your products or services. In this chapter, we'll explore some of the most popular PPC platforms, their unique features, and considerations for choosing the right one for your advertising campaigns.

1. Google Ads

Overview: Google Ads, formerly known as Google AdWords, is the most widely used PPC platform globally. It allows you to display ads on Google's search engine results pages (SERPs) and across its vast network of partner websites and apps.

Key Features:

- **Keyword-Based Advertising:** Bid on keywords relevant to your business and create text or display ads that appear when users search for those keywords.

- **Ad Extensions:** Enhance your ads with site links, callout extensions, structured snippets, and more to provide additional information.
- **Remarketing:** Target previous website visitors with tailored ads to encourage them to return and convert.
- **YouTube Advertising:** Run video ads on YouTube, reaching a massive audience through video content.
- **Audience Targeting:** Utilize various audience targeting options, including demographics, interests, and behavior.

Considerations: Google Ads offers a broad reach and extensive targeting options but can be competitive and expensive for certain industries and keywords.

2. Bing Ads (Microsoft Advertising)

Overview: Bing Ads, now part of Microsoft Advertising, allows you to advertise on the Bing search engine and its network, including Yahoo and AOL.

Key Features:

- **Keyword Advertising:** Similar to Google Ads, bid on keywords and display ads in search results and partner websites.
- **Audience Network:** Extend your reach to Microsoft-owned properties, such as Outlook and LinkedIn, and their partner sites.

- **Remarketing:** Retarget visitors who have interacted with your website using tailored ads.
- **Import from Google Ads:** Easily import your existing Google Ads campaigns into Microsoft Advertising.

Considerations: Bing Ads typically has lower competition and lower cost-per-click (CPC) compared to Google Ads, making it an attractive option for some businesses.

3. Facebook Ads

Overview: Facebook Ads allows you to create and display ads on the world's largest social media platform, including Instagram and Audience Network.

Key Features:

- **Demographic Targeting:** Precisely target users based on demographics, interests, behavior, and even specific life events.
- **Ad Formats:** Choose from a variety of ad formats, including image ads, video ads, carousel ads, and more.
- **Custom Audiences:** Build custom audiences using your existing customer data, website visitors, or app users.
- **Lookalike Audiences:** Expand your reach by targeting users who resemble your existing customers.
- **Messenger Ads:** Engage with users through Messenger chatbots and ads.

Considerations: Facebook Ads offers robust audience targeting options and is especially effective for businesses with visually appealing products or content.

4. LinkedIn Ads

Overview: LinkedIn Ads focuses on professional networking and allows businesses to target a B2B audience.

Key Features:

- **Professional Targeting:** Reach users based on their job titles, company, industry, and professional interests.
- **Sponsored Content:** Promote content such as articles, videos, and posts to a professional audience.
- **Lead Generation Forms:** Collect leads directly within the LinkedIn platform, streamlining the conversion process.
- **InMail Ads:** Send personalized messages to targeted LinkedIn users.

Considerations: LinkedIn Ads is ideal for businesses in the B2B sector looking to connect with a professional audience.

5. Pinterest Ads

Overview: Pinterest Ads allows businesses to promote visually appealing content and products to a primarily female and visually oriented audience.

Key Features:

- **Promoted Pins:** Highlight your pins to appear in users' feeds and search results.
- **Shopping Ads:** Showcase products with shopping-specific pins and reach users looking for purchase inspiration.
- **Audience Targeting:** Target users based on interests, keywords, and demographics.

Considerations: Pinterest Ads is a valuable platform for businesses in the fashion, home decor, and lifestyle industries.

Conclusion

Selecting the right PPC platform depends on your target audience, advertising goals, and budget. Each platform offers unique features and audiences, so consider your business's specific needs when choosing the most suitable platform for your advertising campaigns. Experimentation and ongoing optimization are essential to maximizing the effectiveness of your PPC efforts on any platform.

11

Leveraging Social Media

In today's digital landscape, social media has become a powerful tool for driving website traffic, engaging with your audience, and ultimately generating leads. In this chapter, we'll explore the strategies and tactics for effectively leveraging social media as part of your lead generation efforts.

The Social Media Landscape

Social media platforms have evolved from places where people connect and share to dynamic marketplaces where businesses can connect with their target audience. Each platform has its unique characteristics and audience demographics, so it's essential to choose the right platforms that align with your business and target audience.

Here are some popular social media platforms and their key features:

1. **Facebook:** The largest social media platform with a broad user base. It offers robust advertising options and is

suitable for various businesses.

2. **Instagram:** Known for its visual content, Instagram is ideal for businesses with visually appealing products or services.

3. **Twitter (now "X") :** A platform for real-time updates and engaging with an audience through short, concise messages.

4. **LinkedIn:** Primarily a professional networking platform, LinkedIn is suitable for B2B lead generation and networking.

5. **Pinterest:** Effective for businesses with a visual or lifestyle-oriented focus.

6. **YouTube:** The leading platform for video content, suitable for businesses that can create informative or entertaining videos.

Social Media Lead Generation Strategies

To effectively leverage social media for lead generation, consider the following strategies:

1. **Content Sharing:** Share valuable content from your website, such as blog posts, videos, and infographics, on your social media profiles. These posts should include compelling CTAs and links back to your website for lead capture.

2. **Engagement:** Actively engage with your social media audience by responding to comments, questions, and messages. Encourage conversations and build relationships.

3. **Social Advertising:** Use paid advertising on social media platforms to target specific demographics, interests, and behaviors. Create ad campaigns that direct users to landing pages for lead capture.

4. **Contests and Giveaways:** Run contests and giveaways on social media with the condition that participants provide their contact information to enter. This can rapidly increase your lead database.
5. **Influencer Marketing:** Collaborate with influencers in your industry to promote your products or services. Their endorsements can introduce your brand to a broader audience.
6. **LinkedIn Lead Generation Forms:** Utilize LinkedIn's lead generation forms to collect contact information directly from users who engage with your sponsored content.

Consistency and Authenticity

Consistency in posting, branding, and messaging across your social media channels is crucial for building trust and recognition with your audience. Be authentic in your interactions and provide value in your social media content. Remember that social media is a two-way communication channel, so actively listen to your audience and adjust your strategies based on their feedback.

In the upcoming chapters, we'll delve deeper into other lead generation strategies, such as email marketing, conversion rate optimization (CRO), and effective lead capture techniques. Social media is a dynamic and valuable channel for reaching and engaging with potential leads, and when integrated with your overall lead generation strategy, it can yield significant results.

12

Email Marketing and Lead Nurturing

Email marketing is a powerful tool for nurturing leads and converting them into loyal customers. In this chapter, we'll explore how to effectively use email marketing as a key component of your lead generation strategy.

The Role of Email Marketing in Lead Generation

Email marketing is not just about sending promotional messages; it's a means of building and maintaining relationships with your leads and customers. When done right, it can be one of the most cost-effective methods for converting leads into paying customers.

Here are some key functions of email marketing in lead generation:

1. **Lead Capture:** Collect email addresses through various touchpoints on your website, such as sign-up forms, landing pages, and content downloads.
2. **Lead Nurturing:** Use email sequences to provide valuable

content, insights, and personalized experiences that guide leads through the sales funnel.

3. **Conversion:** Send targeted offers and calls to action (CTAs) to encourage leads to take action, such as making a purchase or requesting a demo.

4. **Customer Retention:** Continue engaging with existing customers to maintain brand loyalty, upsell, or cross-sell products or services.

Building Your Email List

The success of your email marketing efforts depends on the quality and size of your email list. Here are some effective ways to build your email list:

1. **Content Upgrades:** Offer valuable content upgrades, such as ebooks, checklists, or templates, in exchange for users' email addresses.

2. **Newsletter Sign-Up:** Prominently feature a newsletter sign-up form on your website, inviting visitors to stay updated and receive relevant content.

3. **Exit-Intent Pop-Ups:** Use exit-intent pop-ups to capture the email addresses of users who are about to leave your site.

4. **Social Media Promotion:** Promote your email sign-up form on your social media profiles to reach a wider audience.

5. **Contests and Giveaways:** Run contests or giveaways that require participants to provide their email addresses to enter.

Segmentation and Personalization

Segmentation and personalization are critical aspects of effective email marketing. By segmenting your email list based on factors such as demographics, behaviors, and interests, you can send highly targeted and relevant content to different groups of leads.

Personalization involves addressing recipients by their names, tailoring content to their preferences, and sending customized offers or recommendations. Personalized emails tend to have higher open and click-through rates.

Automated Email Campaigns

Automation is a powerful feature of email marketing platforms. You can set up automated email campaigns that trigger based on user actions or specific timelines. Some examples of automated email campaigns include:

- Welcome series for new subscribers.
- Abandoned cart recovery emails.
- Drip campaigns that gradually introduce leads to your products or services.
- Lead nurturing sequences that guide leads through the sales funnel.

Testing and Optimization

Regularly test and optimize your email marketing campaigns. A/B testing can help you determine what subject lines, email content, and CTAs resonate best with your audience. Analyze open rates, click-through rates, conversion rates, and unsubscribe rates to refine your strategies.

In the upcoming chapters, we'll explore further strategies for optimizing lead generation, including conversion rate optimization (CRO), landing page design, and lead capture techniques. Email marketing is a crucial tool for building and nurturing relationships with leads, making it a vital component of your overall lead generation strategy.

13

Conversion Rate Optimization (CRO)

Conversion Rate Optimization (CRO) is the process of systematically improving your website's performance in converting visitors into leads or customers. In this chapter, we'll explore the principles and techniques of CRO to maximize the effectiveness of your lead generation efforts.

Understanding Conversion Rate

Conversion rate is a critical metric in digital marketing. It represents the percentage of website visitors who take a desired action, such as signing up for a newsletter, making a purchase, or requesting more information. A high conversion rate indicates that your website is effectively persuading visitors to become leads or customers.

The formula for calculating conversion rate is:

Conversion Rate=(Number of Conversions/Number of Visitors)×100

The CRO Process

Effective CRO involves a systematic approach to improving your website's conversion performance. Here's a step-by-step process to guide your efforts:

1. **Define Your Conversion Goals:** Begin by identifying the specific actions you want visitors to take on your website. These could include filling out a contact form, making a purchase, subscribing to a newsletter, or requesting a demo.

2. **Analyze User Behavior:** Use analytics tools to gain insights into how visitors interact with your website. Identify drop-off points in the conversion funnel and areas where visitors are struggling.

3. **Hypothesize and Test:** Formulate hypotheses about what might be preventing visitors from converting. These could be related to design, messaging, usability, or trust factors. Test variations of web pages or elements to see which ones improve conversion rates.

4. **A/B Testing:** Conduct A/B tests to compare the performance of different page variations. For example, you might test two different versions of a landing page with different headlines or CTAs to determine which one generates more conversions.

5. **Multivariate Testing:** Experiment with multiple changes on a single page to discover the optimal combination of elements for higher conversions.

6. **Implement Changes:** Based on the results of your tests, implement the changes that lead to improved conversion rates. This might involve redesigning pages, rewriting content, or adjusting the placement of CTAs.

7. **Continuous Optimization:** CRO is an ongoing process. Continuously monitor your website's performance and repeat the testing and optimization cycle to maintain and improve conversion rates.

Key CRO Strategies

Here are some key strategies and tactics to consider when optimizing for conversion:

1. **Clear and Compelling CTAs:** Ensure that your calls to action (CTAs) are prominent, visually appealing, and clearly communicate the value of taking action.
2. **Simplified Forms:** Streamline lead capture forms by reducing the number of fields and making them user-friendly.
3. **Trust Signals:** Display trust-building elements such as customer testimonials, security badges, and privacy assurances to instill confidence in visitors.
4. **Page Load Speed:** Optimize page load times to prevent visitor frustration and abandonment.
5. **Mobile Optimization:** Ensure that your website is fully responsive and user-friendly on mobile devices.
6. **Consistent Messaging:** Maintain a consistent message throughout the user journey, from ads to landing pages to confirmation emails.
7. **Exit-Intent Pop-Ups:** Use exit-intent pop-ups to offer a last-minute incentive or capture leads as visitors are about to leave your site.
8. **Social Proof:** Highlight social proof elements, such as the number of satisfied customers or user-generated content, to boost credibility.

By systematically analyzing and improving the conversion process on your website, you can increase the number of leads you generate from your existing traffic, ultimately driving business growth and success.

In the following chapters, we'll explore more strategies and tactics for lead generation, including landing page design, lead capture techniques, analytics, and ROI measurement. CRO is a crucial component of your lead generation strategy, ensuring that your website effectively converts visitors into valuable leads.

14

Lead Capture and Management

Effective lead capture and management are fundamental to the success of your lead generation efforts. In this chapter, we'll explore strategies and best practices for capturing leads on your website and managing them to drive conversions.

Lead Capture Forms

Lead capture forms are a primary tool for gathering contact information from website visitors. Whether it's a simple newsletter sign-up or a comprehensive request for a quote form, the design and placement of these forms can significantly impact your lead generation.

Key considerations for lead capture forms include:

1. **Form Length:** Keep forms as short as possible while collecting the essential information you need. Longer forms may deter potential leads.
2. **Clear and Relevant Labels:** Use clear and concise labels for form fields. Ensure that users understand the purpose of

each field.

3. **Progressive Profiling:** If you require more information over time, consider using progressive profiling. This technique collects additional details with each subsequent interaction.

4. **Visual Design:** Make forms visually appealing and easy to navigate. Use contrasting colors for buttons and error messages.

5. **Positioning:** Place lead capture forms strategically on your website, such as on landing pages, blog posts, and exit-intent pop-ups.

6. **CTAs:** Use compelling calls to action (CTAs) to encourage form submissions. CTAs should convey the value of taking action.

7. **Validation and Error Handling:** Implement real-time validation to help users complete forms correctly. Provide clear error messages if there are issues with form submissions.

Lead Magnet Offers

Enticing visitors to provide their contact information often requires offering something of value in return. These offers, known as lead magnets, can include:

- Ebooks and guides
- Whitepapers and research reports
- Webinars or online courses
- Templates and checklists
- Discounts or promotional codes
- Exclusive access to content or resources

The choice of lead magnet should align with your target audience's needs and interests.

Lead Scoring and Segmentation

Not all leads are created equal. Implement lead scoring to assign values to leads based on their behavior and attributes. Leads with higher scores indicate a greater likelihood of converting into customers.

Segment your leads based on criteria like demographics, behaviors, and engagement levels. Segmentation allows you to send personalized content and offers to specific groups, increasing the likelihood of conversion.

Lead Nurturing

Once you've captured leads, it's crucial to nurture them through the sales funnel. Create automated lead nurturing sequences that deliver relevant content and offers at the right time. Nurture leads with educational content, product information, and tailored recommendations.

CRM Systems

Customer Relationship Management (CRM) systems are valuable tools for managing leads and tracking interactions. They help you organize lead data, monitor lead status, and streamline communication with leads.

Popular CRM systems include Salesforce, HubSpot CRM, and Zoho CRM. Choose one that aligns with your needs and integrates seamlessly with your lead generation tools.

Lead Follow-Up and Sales Alignment

Timely lead follow-up is critical. Establish processes for sales teams to follow up with leads promptly, whether through email, phone calls, or other communication channels. Align sales and marketing efforts to ensure a seamless transition from lead generation to sales conversion.

In the upcoming chapters, we'll explore additional lead generation strategies, analytics and tracking, and measuring ROI. Effective lead capture and management are essential for maximizing the value of your website's traffic and turning it into a reliable source of business growth.

15

Analytics and Data-Driven Optimization

To make informed decisions and continuously improve your lead generation efforts, you need to rely on data and analytics. In this chapter, we'll explore the importance of analytics and how to use data-driven insights for optimization.

Why Analytics Matters in Lead Generation

Analytics provide valuable insights into how your lead generation efforts are performing. By collecting and analyzing data, you can:

1. **Measure Success:** Determine which lead generation strategies are working and which ones need improvement.
2. **Identify Bottlenecks:** Pinpoint areas in your conversion funnel where leads are dropping off or encountering issues.
3. **Understand User Behavior:** Gain insights into how visitors interact with your website, where they spend their time, and what content resonates with them.
4. **Optimize Campaigns:** Fine-tune your marketing campaigns based on data, allocating resources to the most

effective channels and strategies.

5. **Personalize Experiences:** Use data to segment your audience and deliver personalized content and offers.

Key Analytics Metrics

Several key metrics are essential for assessing the performance of your lead generation efforts:

1. **Conversion Rate:** The percentage of visitors who take a desired action, such as signing up, downloading, or making a purchase.
2. **Click-Through Rate (CTR):** The percentage of users who click on a specific link, often used to measure the performance of email campaigns or online ads.
3. **Bounce Rate:** The percentage of visitors who leave your website after viewing only one page, indicating a lack of engagement.
4. **Time on Page:** How long visitors spend on a particular webpage, which can indicate their level of interest.
5. **Traffic Sources:** Insights into where your website traffic is coming from, including organic search, paid search, social media, and referrals.
6. **Conversion Funnel Analysis:** Tracking user progression through different stages of the conversion process to identify drop-off points.

A/B Testing and Experimentation

A/B testing, also known as split testing, involves comparing two versions (A and B) of a webpage or element to determine which one performs better. You can use A/B testing to optimize landing pages, email subject lines, CTAs, and more.

Experimentation allows you to test hypotheses and make data-driven decisions about changes to your lead generation strategies. For example, you might experiment with different lead magnet offers to see which one attracts more conversions.

Heatmaps and User Session Recordings

Heatmaps and user session recordings provide visual insights into user behavior. Heatmaps show where users click, move, and scroll on your webpages, helping you identify areas of interest or interaction. User session recordings capture actual user interactions, enabling you to see how visitors navigate your website and where they may encounter obstacles.

Marketing Automation and Integration

Leverage marketing automation tools and integrations to streamline data collection and analysis. Many platforms offer built-in analytics and reporting features, making it easier to track the performance of your lead generation campaigns.

Continuous Improvement

Data-driven optimization is an iterative process. Regularly review and analyze your analytics data to identify areas for improvement. Use insights from your data to refine your strategies, experiment with new approaches, and make data-driven decisions.

In the final chapters of this book, we'll explore topics related to measuring the return on investment (ROI) of your lead generation efforts, as well as strategies for long-term success and sustainability. Data-driven optimization is the key to staying competitive and ensuring that your lead generation efforts are effective and efficient.

16

Mobile Optimization for Enhanced Lead Generation

In today's digital landscape, mobile devices play a pivotal role in online activities. As more users access the internet on smartphones and tablets, optimizing your website and lead generation strategies for mobile is not just a preference but a necessity. In this chapter, we'll explore the importance of mobile-friendly websites and mobile-specific lead generation strategies.

The Mobile Revolution

Mobile devices have transformed the way people access information, make purchasing decisions, and engage with online content. Consider these statistics:

- Over half of all web traffic comes from mobile devices, and this number continues to rise.
- Mobile users are more likely to engage with local businesses or make immediate purchase decisions.
- Google uses mobile-friendliness as a ranking factor in

search results, impacting your website's visibility.

Why Mobile Optimization Matters for Lead Generation

1. **User Experience (UX):** A mobile-friendly website ensures a positive user experience. When visitors can easily navigate your site on their mobile devices, they are more likely to engage and convert.
2. **Search Engine Visibility:** Mobile optimization is essential for SEO. Google prioritizes mobile-friendly sites in mobile search results, increasing your website's visibility to potential leads.
3. **Reduced Bounce Rates:** Mobile-optimized sites tend to have lower bounce rates, which means visitors are more likely to explore your content and offers.
4. **Improved Conversions:** A seamless mobile experience can lead to higher conversion rates. Mobile-specific lead generation strategies capitalize on mobile users' preferences and behaviors.

Mobile-Specific Lead Generation Strategies

1. **Responsive Web Design:** Implement responsive web design, which adapts your website's layout and content to various screen sizes. This ensures your site looks and functions well on mobile devices.
2. **Mobile-Friendly Forms:** Optimize lead capture forms for mobile users. Keep forms concise, use large input fields, and avoid unnecessary fields to streamline the submission process.
3. **Click-to-Call Buttons:** Include "click-to-call" buttons

that enable users to contact your business directly with a single tap, making it easier for them to engage.

4. **SMS Marketing:** Utilize SMS marketing to reach mobile users with time-sensitive offers or information. Collect mobile numbers with consent through lead capture forms.

5. **Mobile-Optimized Content:** Craft content that is easily digestible on small screens. Use shorter paragraphs, bullet points, and compelling visuals to engage mobile users.

6. **Geolocation Targeting:** Leverage geolocation data to offer location-based promotions or services to mobile users.

7. **Mobile-Friendly Email Campaigns:** Ensure that your email marketing campaigns and templates are mobile-responsive, as a significant portion of email opens occurs on mobile devices.

Testing and Optimization

Regularly test and optimize your mobile lead generation efforts:

- Conduct mobile usability testing to identify any issues or friction points for mobile users.
- Monitor mobile-specific analytics to track user behavior and conversion rates.
- Use A/B testing to experiment with different mobile-specific elements, such as CTA buttons and form designs.

Conclusion

Mobile optimization is no longer a choice but a necessity for successful lead generation. By creating a mobile-friendly website and implementing mobile-specific lead generation strategies, you can reach and engage with a growing mobile audience effectively. Prioritize user experience, responsiveness, and convenience to maximize the potential of mobile lead generation for your business.

17

Long-Term Strategies for Sustainable Lead Generation

While immediate lead generation is crucial, sustaining your efforts over the long term is equally important for business growth. In this chapter, we'll explore strategies and approaches to maintain a steady flow of leads and ensure your lead generation efforts remain sustainable.

1. Content Marketing for Evergreen Value

Content marketing is a long-term strategy that can provide ongoing value. Create high-quality, evergreen content that continues to attract and engage your target audience over time. This can include in-depth articles, guides, and resources that address common pain points and questions in your industry. Regularly update and optimize your content to keep it relevant and valuable.

2. SEO and Organic Traffic Growth

Invest in long-term search engine optimization (SEO) strategies to improve your website's visibility in search results.

As your website's authority grows, it becomes a consistent source of organic traffic and leads. Focus on creating valuable, keyword-rich content, optimizing on-page elements, and building high-quality backlinks.

3. Email Marketing and Nurturing Relationships

Email marketing is not just about acquiring new leads; it's also about nurturing existing ones. Build and maintain relationships with your email subscribers through personalized content, valuable insights, and special offers. Consistent communication can lead to repeat business, referrals, and long-term customer loyalty.

4. Thought Leadership and Authority Building

Position yourself and your brand as thought leaders in your industry. Share your expertise through articles, blog posts, webinars, and speaking engagements. As you become a trusted source of information, more leads will naturally gravitate toward your business.

5. Social Media Engagement

Maintain an active presence on social media platforms where your target audience congregates. Engage in meaningful conversations, share valuable content, and interact with your followers. Over time, this engagement can lead to a community of loyal followers who become leads and customers.

6. Referral and Word-of-Mouth Marketing

Encourage your satisfied customers to become brand advocates. Implement referral programs and encourage customers to leave positive reviews and refer friends and colleagues. Word-of-mouth marketing can lead to a steady stream of high-quality leads.

7. Partnerships and Collaborations

Explore partnerships and collaborations with other businesses in your industry or complementary niches. Joint ventures, co-marketing campaigns, and cross-promotions can introduce your brand to new audiences and generate leads through shared efforts.

8. Customer Retention and Upselling

Don't forget about your existing customers. Focus on providing exceptional customer experiences, staying in touch, and offering additional products or services that can address their evolving needs. Happy customers can become repeat buyers and refer others.

9. Analytics and Iteration

Continuously monitor and analyze your lead generation efforts. Use data to identify trends, successes, and areas for improvement. Iterate your strategies based on data-driven insights to keep your lead generation efforts effective and efficient.

10. Adapting to Market Changes

Stay adaptable and open to changing market conditions. Be ready to pivot your strategies or explore new channels as industry trends and consumer preferences evolve.

Sustainable lead generation requires a combination of ongoing efforts, strategic planning, and a commitment to delivering value to your audience. By implementing these long-term strategies, you can create a resilient lead generation engine that fuels your business growth for years to come.

18

Essential Tools and Software for Website Lead Generation

Effective lead generation on your website often relies on the use of various tools and software to streamline processes, analyze data, and optimize your strategies. In this chapter, we'll explore some essential tools and software that can help you generate and manage leads more efficiently.

Customer Relationship Management (CRM) Software

Overview: CRM software is essential for managing and nurturing leads throughout the customer journey. It allows you to track interactions, segment leads, and personalize communication.

Key Features:

- **Lead Tracking:** Keep detailed records of leads, including their contact information, interactions, and conversion progress.

- **Email Marketing Integration:** Integrate with email marketing platforms to automate lead nurturing campaigns.
- **Lead Scoring:** Assign scores to leads based on their behavior and engagement, prioritizing high-quality prospects.
- **Reporting and Analytics:** Gain insights into lead conversion rates, sales pipeline, and overall performance.

Popular CRM Tools: Salesforce, HubSpot CRM, Zoho CRM, and Pipedrive.

Marketing Automation Software

Overview: Marketing automation tools enable you to automate repetitive marketing tasks, such as email campaigns, lead nurturing, and lead scoring.

Key Features:

- **Email Marketing Automation:** Create automated email sequences based on user behavior and preferences.
- **Lead Segmentation:** Segment your leads into categories for more personalized communication.
- **Lead Scoring:** Assign scores to leads to identify the most promising prospects.
- **Workflow Automation:** Automate marketing processes and trigger actions based on user interactions.

Popular Marketing Automation Tools: HubSpot Marketing Hub, Marketo, ActiveCampaign, and Mailchimp.

Lead Capture and Forms

Overview: Lead capture tools help you create and optimize lead capture forms on your website, making it easy for visitors to provide their information.

Key Features:

- **Drag-and-Drop Form Builders:** Create custom lead capture forms without coding.
- **A/B Testing:** Experiment with different form designs and fields to optimize conversion rates.
- **Exit-Intent Pop-Ups:** Capture leads when visitors are about to leave your site.
- **Progressive Profiling:** Gradually collect more information about leads over time.

Popular Lead Capture Tools: OptinMonster, Sumo, Convert-Flow, and Leadpages.

Analytics and Heatmapping Tools

Overview: Analytics and heatmapping tools help you understand user behavior on your website, identify areas for improvement, and optimize lead generation efforts.

Key Features:

- **Visitor Tracking:** Track user journeys and behavior, including pages viewed and time spent.

- **Heatmaps:** Visualize where users click, move, and scroll on your webpages.
- **Conversion Funnel Analysis:** Identify drop-off points in your lead generation process.
- **A/B Testing:** Test different elements to improve conversion rates.

Popular Analytics and Heatmapping Tools: Google Analytics, Hotjar, Crazy Egg, and Mixpanel.

Social Proof and FOMO Tools

Overview: Social proof and FOMO (Fear of Missing Out) tools create a sense of urgency and trust among website visitors, encouraging them to take action.

Key Features:

- **Notification Pop-Ups:** Display recent sign-ups, purchases, or actions taken by other users.
- **Countdown Timers:** Create urgency by counting down to special offers or events.
- **Customer Reviews and Ratings:** Showcase positive feedback and ratings from satisfied customers.

Popular Social Proof and FOMO Tools: TrustPulse, ProveSource, Fomo, and NotifyVisitors.

Chatbots and Live Chat Software

Overview: Chatbots and live chat software provide real-time engagement with website visitors, answering questions and capturing leads.

Key Features:

- **Automated Responses:** Chatbots can answer frequently asked questions and collect lead information.
- **Real-Time Support:** Offer immediate assistance to visitors with live chat agents.
- **Lead Capture:** Use chatbots to initiate conversations and collect contact information.

Popular Chatbots and Live Chat Tools: Intercom, Drift, Tawk.to, and LiveChat.

Exit-Intent Technology

Overview: Exit-intent technology detects when a visitor is about to leave your website and triggers a targeted message or offer to encourage them to stay or convert.

Key Features:

- **Exit-Intent Pop-Ups:** Display customized messages, discounts, or lead capture forms when a visitor intends to exit.
- **Behavior Tracking:** Monitor mouse movements and speed to detect exit intent accurately.

Popular Exit-Intent Tools: OptinMonster, Picreel, BounceX (Now Wunderkind), and TrustPulse.

The right tools and software can significantly enhance your website's lead generation capabilities. By leveraging CRM software, marketing automation, lead capture forms, analytics, and other essential tools, you can streamline processes, optimize campaigns, and convert more website visitors into leads. Choose the tools that align with your specific goals and needs to maximize the effectiveness of your lead generation efforts.

19

The Future of Lead Generation:
Emerging Trends and Technologies

The landscape of lead generation is continually evolving, driven by advancements in technology and shifts in consumer behavior. In this chapter, we'll explore emerging trends and technologies that are shaping the future of lead generation.

1. Artificial Intelligence (AI) and Machine Learning

AI and machine learning are transforming lead generation by automating tasks, personalizing user experiences, and predicting customer behavior. AI-powered chatbots and virtual assistants can engage with website visitors in real-time, answer questions, and capture leads. Machine learning algorithms analyze vast amounts of data to identify patterns and optimize marketing strategies for better lead generation results.

2. Voice Search and Conversational Marketing

The rise of voice-activated devices like smart speakers has led to an increase in voice search. Optimizing your content for voice search queries can attract a new audience and generate leads. Additionally, conversational marketing tools like chat-bots and messaging apps enable more natural and interactive interactions with potential leads, enhancing user engagement and capturing contact information.

3. Video Marketing and Live Streaming

Video content continues to gain popularity as a lead generation tool. Creating informative, entertaining, and engaging videos can attract and convert leads. Live streaming on platforms like YouTube, Facebook Live, and Instagram Live allows real-time interaction with your audience, providing opportunities for lead capture and engagement.

4. Personalization and Hyper-Personalization

Personalization has become a standard in lead generation, but hyper-personalization takes it to the next level. Leveraging data and AI, hyper-personalization tailors marketing messages and content to individual users based on their preferences, behaviors, and past interactions. This level of personalization can significantly improve lead conversion rates.

5. Interactive Content and Gamification

Interactive content such as quizzes, polls, assessments, and contests can be powerful lead generation tools. Gamification techniques, like awarding points or prizes for engagement and referrals, encourage users to participate and share their contact information.

6. Privacy and Data Protection

As privacy concerns grow, it's crucial to prioritize data protection and compliance with regulations like GDPR and CCPA. Gain user trust by being transparent about data usage and providing opt-in options. A strong commitment to data security can help maintain and attract leads.

7. Voice and Video Search Optimization

Optimizing your content for voice and video search is becoming increasingly important. Voice assistants like Siri, Google Assistant, and Alexa rely on structured data and clear answers to user queries. Ensure your content provides concise, accurate responses to voice and video search queries.

8. Social Commerce and Shoppable Content

Social media platforms are integrating shopping features, allowing users to purchase products directly from social posts. Shoppable content and social commerce create opportunities for lead generation, particularly if your target audience is active on these platforms.

9. Predictive Analytics and Lead Scoring

Predictive analytics tools use historical data to forecast future lead behavior and identify the most promising leads. Lead scoring models, powered by predictive analytics, help prioritize and focus efforts on leads with the highest likelihood of converting into customers.

10. Augmented Reality (AR) and Virtual Reality (VR)

AR and VR technologies offer immersive experiences that can engage potential leads. For example, AR can be used for virtual try-on experiences for fashion brands, while VR can create virtual tours of real estate properties or interactive product demonstrations.

As you navigate the evolving landscape of lead generation, staying informed about these emerging trends and technologies will be critical to remaining competitive and effectively capturing and nurturing leads in the future. Incorporating these innovations into your lead generation strategy can help you adapt to changing consumer preferences and stay ahead of the curve.

20

Conclusion and Actionable Steps

In this final chapter, we'll summarize the key takeaways from this book and provide you with actionable steps to transform your website into a lead generation machine. Let's review the essential points and outline your next steps.

Key Takeaways:

1. **The Problem of Online Brochures:** Many websites serve as nothing more than online brochures, missing out on the opportunity to capture valuable leads.
2. **Effective Lead Generation:** To turn your website into a lead generation machine, you need to implement strategies that attract, engage, and convert visitors into leads.
3. **Diverse Lead Generation Channels:** Successful lead generation involves a mix of strategies, including content marketing, SEO, social media, email marketing, and more.
4. **Conversion Rate Optimization (CRO):** Continuously optimize your website and landing pages to improve conversion rates and maximize lead generation.

5. **Lead Capture and Management:** Implement effective lead capture forms, segmentation, and lead nurturing to maintain a healthy lead database.

6. **Analytics and ROI:** Regularly measure and analyze your lead generation efforts to calculate ROI and ROMI. Use data to make informed decisions and optimize your strategies.

7. **Long-Term Sustainability:** Implement long-term strategies such as content marketing, SEO, email marketing, and customer retention to sustain lead generation efforts.

8. **Emerging Trends:** Stay updated on emerging trends and technologies like AI, voice search, and personalization to remain competitive in lead generation.

Actionable Steps:

1. **Assessment:** Evaluate your current website and lead generation efforts. Identify areas where improvements are needed.

2. **Set Clear Goals:** Define clear and measurable lead generation goals. What specific actions do you want visitors to take on your website?

3. **Content Strategy:** Develop a content strategy that addresses your target audience's pain points and interests. Create high-quality, valuable content that serves as lead magnets.

4. **SEO Optimization:** Invest in SEO to improve your website's visibility in search results. Conduct keyword research and optimize your content and technical elements.

5. **Social Media Engagement:** Choose the social media platforms most relevant to your audience. Engage with your audience, share content, and use social advertising to

capture leads.

6. **Email Marketing:** Build an email list and create lead nurturing sequences. Segment your email list for personalized communication.

7. **Conversion Rate Optimization:** Continuously optimize your website's design, forms, and CTAs to improve conversion rates. Use A/B testing to experiment with different elements.

8. **Lead Capture Forms:** Implement strategically placed lead capture forms with compelling CTAs. Consider using exit-intent pop-ups for additional lead capture opportunities.

9. **Analytics and Data:** Set up analytics tools to track user behavior, conversion rates, and campaign performance. Regularly review and analyze data to make data-driven decisions.

10. **Long-Term Strategies:** Develop and execute long-term strategies like content marketing, SEO, and customer retention to ensure sustainable lead generation.

11. **Stay Informed:** Stay up-to-date with industry trends and emerging technologies. Experiment with new strategies and tools as they become relevant to your audience.

12. **Privacy and Compliance:** Ensure that your lead generation practices comply with privacy regulations and prioritize data security to build trust with leads.

13. **Collaboration:** Foster collaboration between your marketing and sales teams to ensure a seamless transition from lead generation to conversion.

By taking these actionable steps and consistently implementing the strategies and best practices discussed in this book, you'll be well-equipped to transform your website into a lead generation machine. Remember that lead generation is an ongoing process that requires adaptability and continuous improvement. Keep learning and evolving to stay ahead in the dynamic world of digital marketing.

II

Part Two - Building Your Lead Magnet

21

The Importance of Lead Magnets

In the world of digital marketing, generating leads is the lifeblood of any successful business. Whether you're running a small startup or managing a multinational corporation, the ability to capture and nurture potential customers is essential for sustainable growth. This is where lead magnets come into play.

What Is a Lead Magnet?

A lead magnet is a valuable piece of content or an offer that you provide to your target audience in exchange for their contact information, usually an email address. It serves as a magnet, attracting potential leads and encouraging them to take a specific action, such as subscribing to your email list, downloading a resource, or signing up for a webinar. Essentially, it's an irresistible incentive that entices people to engage with your brand.

Lead magnets are a fundamental component of inbound marketing strategies and play a pivotal role in building relationships with your audience. They are designed to initiate a conversation, allowing you to nurture leads over time and guide them through the sales funnel. Here's why lead magnets are so crucial:

1. **Building a Permission-Based Relationship**: When a prospect willingly shares their contact information in exchange for your lead magnet, they give you permission to communicate with them. This forms the basis of a mutually beneficial relationship where you can provide valuable content, offers, and solutions to their problems.

2. **Qualifying Leads**: Lead magnets help you filter and identify potential customers who are genuinely interested in your products or services. This means you're not wasting time and resources on uninterested or unqualified leads.

3. **Personalization and Targeting**: With contact information in hand, you can personalize your marketing messages and tailor them to the specific needs and preferences of your audience. This personal touch increases the likelihood of conversion.

4. **Education and Trust-Building**: Many lead magnets are educational in nature, providing valuable insights, tips, or solutions to a particular problem. By offering useful information, you demonstrate your expertise and build trust with your audience.

5. **Cost-Effective Marketing**: Compared to traditional advertising methods, lead magnets are cost-effective. They allow you to reach a highly targeted audience without the exorbitant costs associated with mass marketing campaigns.

6. **Measurable Results**: Lead magnets are trackable. You can measure their performance by analyzing conversion rates, click-through rates, and other metrics. This data-driven approach enables you to refine your strategies for better results.

7. **Long-Term Value**: The leads you acquire through effective lead magnets have the potential to become loyal customers who generate revenue for your business over an extended period. Building a solid customer base is essential for long-term success.

As you delve deeper into this book, you'll discover the strategies, tactics, and best practices for creating the ultimate lead magnet that not only captures leads but also nurtures them into paying customers. We'll explore various types of lead magnets, content creation techniques, landing page design, promotion strategies, and much more.

Are you ready to harness the power of lead magnets to super-charge your lead generation efforts? Let's dive in and explore how to create compelling, high-converting lead magnets that will propel your business to new heights.

22

Types of Lead Magnets

Choosing the Right Incentive for Your Audience

Lead magnets come in various forms, and selecting the right type is crucial for attracting and engaging your target audience. In this chapter, we'll explore the different types of lead magnets and provide insights into when to use each one effectively.

eBooks and Whitepapers

Definition: eBooks and whitepapers are in-depth, informative documents that dive deep into a specific topic or problem.

Best For: B2B businesses, industries that require in-depth research or data-driven insights.

Advantages:

- Establishes authority and expertise.

- Appeals to audiences seeking in-depth knowledge.
- Provides value through comprehensive information.

Tips:

- Choose topics that align with your audience's interests.
- Include visual elements to enhance readability.
- Offer actionable solutions or takeaways.

Checklists and Cheat Sheets

Definition: Checklists and cheat sheets are concise lists of steps or guidelines to achieve a specific goal or solve a problem quickly.

Best For: Busy professionals, individuals seeking quick solutions.

Advantages:

- Quick and easy to consume.
- Provides immediate value and actionable steps.
- Appeals to audiences looking for shortcuts or efficiency.

Tips:

- Keep them concise and focused.
- Use clear, actionable language.
- Solve a common pain point or challenge.

Templates and Worksheets

Definition: Templates and worksheets are customizable tools that help users complete a task, plan, or organize information.

Best For: Industries requiring planning, organization, or practical tools.

Advantages:

- Promotes engagement and interactivity.
- Helps users apply concepts to their specific situation.
- Provides a tangible resource with ongoing value.

Tips:

- Ensure they are user-friendly and easy to customize.
- Focus on solving a specific problem.
- Include instructions or guidance.

Webinars and Video Courses

Definition: Webinars and video courses are live or recorded multimedia presentations that educate and engage the audience on a particular topic.

Best For: Industries where visual and auditory learning is effective, complex subjects.

Advantages:

- Allows for direct engagement with the audience.
- Provides in-depth, visual explanations.
- Builds a sense of community.

Tips:

- Promote well in advance to maximize attendance.
- Encourage audience interaction during live sessions.
- Offer recordings for those who can't attend live.

Quizzes and Assessments

Definition: Quizzes and assessments are interactive tools that help users evaluate their knowledge, skills, or needs.

Best For: Industries that can benefit from personalized recommendations, self-assessment.

Advantages:

- Encourages active participation.
- Provides personalized results and recommendations.
- Segments your audience based on their responses.

Tips:

- Create engaging, well-designed quizzes.
- Offer valuable insights or solutions based on quiz results.
- Keep them concise to maintain user interest.

Discounts and Promotions

Definition: Discounts and promotions offer users a special deal or exclusive access to products or services.

Best For: E-commerce businesses, businesses looking to boost sales or conversion rates.

Advantages:

- Drives immediate action.
- Appeals to price-sensitive consumers.
- Encourages first-time purchases.

Tips:

- Clearly communicate the value of the discount.
- Set clear expiration dates to create urgency.
- Use personalized offers when possible.

Case Studies and Success Stories

Definition: Case studies and success stories showcase real-life examples of how your products or services solved a problem or delivered results.

Best For: Businesses looking to build trust and credibility, industries with a longer sales cycle.

Advantages:

- Provides social proof and credibility.
- Demonstrates tangible benefits.
- Appeals to prospects seeking validation.

Tips:

- Choose relatable and compelling stories.
- Highlight measurable results and outcomes.
- Use storytelling techniques for maximum impact.

Tools and Resources

Definition: Tools and resources offer access to valuable online or downloadable tools, such as calculators, generators, or software.

Best For: Industries that can offer practical tools, businesses looking to automate processes or provide value through technology.

Advantages:

- Offers immediate utility.
- Positions your brand as a valuable resource.
- Encourages repeat visits and engagement.

Tips:

- Ensure the tools are user-friendly.
- Highlight unique features or benefits.
- Provide clear instructions for use.

In the following chapters, we'll delve deeper into each type of lead magnet, providing guidance on how to create and implement them effectively. By choosing the right lead magnet for your audience and business goals, you can significantly increase your chances of capturing and nurturing valuable leads.

23

Landing Page Design

Creating an Irresistible Gateway to Your Lead Magnet

Your lead magnet's landing page serves as the gateway that connects your audience with your valuable content. In this chapter, we'll explore the essential elements of a well-designed landing page that converts visitors into leads.

The Elements of an Effective Landing Page

1. **Attention-Grabbing Headlines and Subheadings**: The headline should immediately convey the value of your lead magnet. Use clear, concise language, and make it compelling. Subheadings can provide additional context and entice visitors to keep reading.

2. **Persuasive Copywriting**: Your landing page copy should be persuasive and focused on benefits. Explain how your lead magnet solves a problem or fulfills a need. Use persuasive language to encourage action.

3. **Clear Call-to-Action (CTA)**: Your CTA is the action you want visitors to take, such as "Download Now" or "Sign Up." Make it highly visible and use contrasting colors to draw attention. It should be concise and action-oriented.

4. **Visually Appealing Design**: A clean and visually appealing design is essential. Use high-quality images and graphics that align with your brand. Ensure that the layout is user-friendly and easy to navigate.

5. **Benefit-Oriented Bullet Points**: Use bullet points to high-light the key benefits of your lead magnet. What will visitors gain by downloading or accessing it? Make it clear and concise.

6. **Social Proof**: Display testimonials, reviews, or logos of trusted organizations or partners. Social proof builds credibility and trust. People are more likely to take action when they see that others have benefited.

7. **Privacy and Trust Seals**: Assure visitors that their information is secure. Display privacy policy links and trust seals (e.g., SSL certificates) to instill confidence in your site's security.

8. **Minimal Distractions**: Remove unnecessary distractions from the landing page. Avoid clutter, excessive links, or unrelated content that might divert visitors' attention.

9. **Mobile Responsiveness**: Ensure that your landing page is mobile-responsive. Many visitors will access it from smartphones or tablets, and a mobile-friendly design is essential for a seamless experience.

10. **Form and Opt-In Mechanism**: If your lead magnet requires contact information, keep the form fields simple and request only essential information. Use clear labels and make the opt-in process as frictionless as possible.

Landing Page Best Practices

1. Single Focus: Each landing page should have a single, clear goal. Don't dilute your message with multiple offers or distractions.

2. A/B Testing: Experiment with different elements, such as headline variations, CTA button colors, or form fields, and use A/B testing to determine which versions perform best.

3. Compelling Visuals: Use visuals strategically to complement your message. Images of the lead magnet or happy customers can enhance the page's appeal.

4. Consistent Branding: Ensure that your landing page design aligns with your brand's visual identity and messaging.

5. Clear Value Proposition: Clearly communicate what visitors will gain from your lead magnet. Why should they take action?

6. Mobile Optimization: Test your landing page on various devices to ensure it looks and functions well on all screen sizes.

7. Analytics and Tracking: Implement analytics tools to track visitor behavior and conversions. Monitor your landing page's performance and make adjustments accordingly.

8. Loading Speed: Optimize page load times to prevent visitors from bouncing due to slow loading.

9. Thank-You Page: After users complete the desired action,

direct them to a thank-you page that confirms their action and provides additional instructions or resources.

Building Trust and Encouraging Action

An effective landing page not only captures visitors' attention but also builds trust and guides them toward taking action. It's the bridge that connects your lead magnet with potential leads. In the next chapter, we'll explore lead magnet promotion strategies to drive traffic to your landing page and maximize its impact.

24

Lead Magnet Promotion

Strategies to Drive Traffic to Your Landing Page

Creating a compelling lead magnet and a well-designed landing page is only half the battle. To maximize your lead generation efforts, you need to effectively promote your lead magnet and drive targeted traffic to your landing page. In this chapter, we'll explore various strategies for lead magnet promotion.

Social Media Marketing

Social media platforms offer a powerful way to connect with your audience and promote your lead magnet. Here are some key strategies:

1. **Regular Posting**: Share teasers, snippets, or related content on your social media profiles to generate interest. Use eye-catching visuals and compelling captions.

2. **Paid Advertising**: Consider running targeted ad campaigns on platforms like Facebook, Instagram, and LinkedIn. Use the platforms' ad targeting features to reach your ideal audience.

3. **Influencer Collaboration**: Partner with influencers or industry experts who can promote your lead magnet to their followers. Influencers can provide credibility and access to a wider audience.

4. **Social Sharing**: Make it easy for visitors to share your landing page on their own social media profiles. Include social sharing buttons on your thank-you page.

Email Marketing Campaigns

Leveraging your email list is an effective way to promote your lead magnet. Here's how:

1. **Segmentation**: Segment your email list based on the interests and preferences of your subscribers. Send targeted emails promoting your lead magnet to relevant segments.

2. **Dedicated Email**: Send a dedicated email to your subscribers, highlighting the value of your lead magnet and providing a direct link to the landing page.

3. **Autoresponders**: Create automated email sequences that introduce your lead magnet and nurture leads over time. Use a series of emails to build anticipation.

Content Marketing

Content marketing can drive organic traffic to your landing page. Consider these tactics:

1. **Blog Posts**: Write blog posts related to the topic of your lead magnet and include calls-to-action (CTAs) that lead to your landing page.

2. **Guest Blogging**: Contribute guest posts to industry-related websites or blogs and include links to your lead magnet landing page in your author bio or within the content.

3. **SEO Optimization**: Optimize your landing page and related content for search engines. Use relevant keywords and meta tags to improve visibility in search results.

4. **Video Marketing**: Create informative videos that touch on the subject of your lead magnet. Promote the video and include links to your landing page in video descriptions.

Paid Advertising

Paid advertising can deliver immediate traffic to your landing page. Consider these options:

1. **Google Ads**: Use Google Ads to target specific keywords related to your lead magnet. Create compelling ad copy and landing page content.

2. **Social Media Ads**: Run paid ad campaigns on social media

platforms, targeting your desired audience based on demographics, interests, and behavior.

3. **Display Advertising**: Invest in display advertising on relevant websites or platforms. Banner ads can increase visibility and drive traffic.

Collaboration and Partnerships

Collaborating with others can expand your reach and credibility:

1. **Cross-Promotion**: Partner with complementary businesses or brands to cross-promote each other's lead magnets to your respective audiences.

2. **Joint Webinars or Workshops**: Host webinars or workshops with industry experts or influencers, where your lead magnet is a featured resource.

3. **Affiliate Partnerships**: Set up an affiliate program where others promote your lead magnet in exchange for a commission for each lead generated.

SEO and Organic Traffic

Long-term visibility in search engines can bring consistent traffic to your landing page:

1. **Content Updates**: Regularly update and expand the content related to your lead magnet to keep it fresh and relevant.

2. **Backlink Building**: Work on building high-quality backlinks to your landing page from reputable websites within your industry.

3. **Social Sharing**: Encourage social sharing of your lead magnet. When people share it, it can lead to more organic traffic.

Analyzing and Adjusting

Regardless of the promotion strategies you use, it's essential to analyze the results and make adjustments:

1. **Conversion Tracking**: Monitor your landing page's conversion rate and traffic sources. Identify what's working and what needs improvement.

2. **A/B Testing**: Continuously test different elements of your landing page and promotional campaigns to optimize for better results.

3. **Feedback and Iteration**: Gather feedback from users and leads. Use this feedback to make improvements to your lead magnet and promotion strategies.

4. **Scaling Successful Campaigns**: If a specific promotion strategy is highly effective, consider scaling it up to reach a larger audience.

By implementing these lead magnet promotion strategies and continuously refining your approach, you can drive targeted traffic to your landing page, capture more leads, and ultimately grow your business.

In the next chapter, we'll explore the critical aspects of lead capture and data collection, ensuring that you make the most of the leads you've generated.

25

Lead Capture and Data Collection

Maximizing the Value of Your Leads

Congratulations! You've successfully driven traffic to your landing page and captured the attention of potential leads. Now, it's time to focus on collecting and managing the data that will help you nurture these leads into loyal customers. In this chapter, we'll explore lead capture and data collection strategies.

Forms and Opt-In Mechanisms

Forms are the primary means by which you collect lead information on your landing page. Here's how to optimize them:

1. **Keep It Simple**: Request only essential information, such as name and email address. Lengthy forms can deter potential leads.

2. **Clear Labels and Instructions**: Use clear, concise labels for

form fields. Provide instructions, if necessary, to guide users through the process.

3. **Progressive Profiling**: If you need more detailed information, consider using progressive profiling. Collect additional data in subsequent interactions with the lead.

4. **Multi-Step Forms**: For longer forms, break them into multiple steps to make them appear less intimidating. Use a progress indicator to show users how far they've come.

5. **Visual Cues**: Use visual cues, such as asterisks (*), to indicate required fields. This reduces confusion and ensures users complete the necessary information.

GDPR Compliance and Privacy

Ensure that your lead capture process complies with data privacy regulations, such as the General Data Protection Regulation (GDPR) in Europe. Here's what to consider:

1. **Consent**: Clearly communicate why you're collecting data and obtain explicit consent from users to use their information for specific purposes.

2. **Privacy Policy**: Link to your privacy policy on your landing page and explain how you handle user data. Include information on data retention and user rights.

3. **Opt-In and Opt-Out**: Allow users to opt in or out of email communications. Provide an easy way for them to unsubscribe

from your emails at any time.

4. **Data Security**: Implement security measures to protect user data. Use encryption and secure data storage methods to prevent breaches.

5. **Data Access**: Be prepared to provide users with access to their data upon request. Have a process in place to handle data access and deletion requests.

Email Marketing Integration

Integrating your lead capture forms with your email marketing platform streamlines lead management. Here's how to make the most of this integration:

1. **Autoresponders**: Set up autoresponder email sequences to deliver the lead magnet and begin nurturing leads immediately after they opt in.

2. **Segmentation**: Use the data you collect to segment your email list. Send targeted content and offers based on users' interests and behavior.

3. **Lead Scoring**: Implement lead scoring to prioritize and identify high-potential leads. Focus your efforts on those who are more likely to convert.

4. **Personalization**: Personalize your email campaigns based on the information you gather. Address leads by their names and tailor content to their preferences.

5. **Drip Campaigns**: Create drip campaigns that deliver a series of emails over time. Gradually introduce leads to your products or services.

Analytics and Tracking

Data analysis is crucial for optimizing your lead generation efforts. Consider the following:

1. **Conversion Tracking**: Monitor conversion rates on your landing page. Identify which traffic sources and campaigns are most effective.

2. **Email Performance**: Track email open rates, click-through rates, and engagement metrics to refine your email marketing strategies.

3. **Lead Source Attribution**: Understand where your leads are coming from. This helps you allocate resources to the most productive channels.

4. **A/B Testing**: Continuously test different elements of your lead capture forms and email campaigns to improve results.

5. **Lead Nurturing Metrics**: Measure the progression of leads through your sales funnel. Identify bottlenecks and areas for improvement.

Continuous Improvement

Effective lead capture and data collection are ongoing processes. To maximize the value of your leads, commit to continuous improvement:

1. **Feedback Loop**: Gather feedback from your leads to understand their needs and preferences. Use this information to refine your strategies.

2. **Data Cleansing**: Regularly clean and update your lead database to ensure accuracy and relevance.

3. **CRM Integration**: Consider integrating a Customer Relationship Management (CRM) system to better manage and track leads through the entire sales cycle.

4. **Lead Nurturing**: Develop and refine lead nurturing workflows to move leads from awareness to conversion.

By optimizing your lead capture and data collection processes, you can extract the maximum value from the leads you generate. In the next chapter, we'll explore strategies for analyzing and optimizing your lead generation efforts to achieve even better results.

26

Conclusion and Roadmap

Building the Ultimate Lead Magnet and Lead Generation System

Congratulations on reaching the final chapter of this book on building the ultimate lead magnet and lead generation system. By now, you've gained a comprehensive understanding of the strategies and tactics necessary to create an effective lead generation system. Let's recap the key takeaways and provide you with a roadmap to success.

Key Takeaways

Throughout this book, we've covered a range of important topics related to lead generation. Here are the key takeaways:

1. **Understanding Your Audience**: Begin by understanding your target audience and creating detailed buyer personas. This knowledge will guide your lead magnet creation.

2. **Types of Lead Magnets**: There are various types of lead magnets, including eBooks, checklists, webinars, and more. Choose the type that best suits your audience and goals.
3. **Compelling Content**: Craft compelling content for your lead magnet. It should be high-quality, relevant, and solve a specific problem for your audience.
4. **Landing Page Design**: Your landing page is the gateway to your lead magnet. Design it effectively with attention-grabbing headlines, persuasive copy, and clear CTAs.
5. **Lead Magnet Promotion**: Use various strategies, such as social media marketing, email marketing, content marketing, paid advertising, and collaboration, to drive traffic to your landing page.
6. **Lead Capture and Data Collection**: Create user-friendly forms for lead capture and ensure GDPR compliance. Integrate with email marketing platforms to manage leads effectively.
7. **Analyzing and Optimizing**: Monitor key performance indicators (KPIs), conduct A/B testing, and continuously optimize your lead generation efforts for better results.

Your Roadmap to Success

Now that you've absorbed all this knowledge, it's time to put it into action. Here's a roadmap to help you build the ultimate lead magnet and lead generation system:

Step 1: Define Your Audience

· Conduct thorough audience research.

- Create detailed buyer personas.

Step 2: Choose Your Lead Magnet Type

- Select the type of lead magnet that aligns with your audience's preferences and your business goals.

Step 3: Craft Compelling Content

- Develop high-quality content that addresses your audience's pain points and provides valuable solutions.

Step 4: Design an Effective Landing Page

- Create an attention-grabbing landing page with persuasive copy and clear CTAs.

Step 5: Promote Your Lead Magnet

- Implement a mix of promotion strategies, including social media, email marketing, content marketing, paid advertising, and collaboration.

Step 6: Capture Leads and Data

- Design user-friendly forms and ensure GDPR compliance.
- Integrate with email marketing platforms for efficient lead management.

Step 7: Analyze and Optimize

- Monitor KPIs to track performance.
- Conduct A/B testing to improve conversion rates.
- Continuously optimize your strategies for better results.

Step 8: Scale and Adapt

- Scale successful campaigns to reach a larger audience.
- Stay updated on industry trends and adapt your strategies accordingly.

Step 9: Nurture Leads

- Implement lead nurturing workflows to guide leads through the sales funnel.

Step 10: Evaluate and Iterate

- Regularly evaluate your lead generation efforts and gather feedback from your team and leads.
- Iterate and refine your strategies for continuous improvement.

Remember, building the ultimate lead magnet and lead generation system is an ongoing process. It requires dedication, adaptability, and a commitment to providing value to your audience. By following this roadmap and staying focused on your goals, you can achieve sustainable growth and success in your business.

Thank you for reading this book, and I wish you the best of luck in your lead generation endeavors!

Printed in Great Britain
by Amazon

29660218R00066